OGIE  Mouse  BLOB
hands
ALON
BBO  Dingo Boingo  WA
TAPP
FEEP  BIDR
EOWING  Helena Rubinstein  DE
TUP  HO-PO  SCRUNDLE  GOMES  PANTHER  BUTTER PELICA
STEAK
OLATER  portney  LONELY OTTER  GLOUPTIN  pyune
TSYDUTSY  Gritchies  WASH  FOOFER  SKONK  CANTEE-
MEDALS
UZUNDER  PURPURS  TOSH  DOOT  The Quincy
VEITATE  The Camel Effect  DOOT,  FLOOPIE  BL
ANG  APTERP!  Condoleezza Rice  FREEDOM  deenje  GEEDUN
en milk  BURGER  ERUBIE  portney
GARBOON!  TILLY  BOBBO  FEEP  Dingo
AVE  SMOT  Gutterstretch  TAPPY  Boingo
EEPS  BUTTER PELICAN  LONELY OTTER  BIDRAH!  PURPURS
H  Helena Rubinstein  SKONK  pyune  FOOFER  Broccoli
Nuts
SH  GRETZKY  Mouse  GOMES  GARBOON
HER  SCRUNDLE  hands  GLOUPTIN  TOLATER  The Qu
AK  FLOOPIE  FEEP  ERUBIE  Condoleezza Rice  ERUBIE  The Q
etch  chicken milk  PANTHER  Gritchies  BLORB  FREEDON
LY  STEAK  SKONK  TWAIF  FUTSYDUT
portney  SCRUNDLE

GOOGLE Mouse BLORP Gutterstretch BEEPS TILL
ASHALON hands WARMIES Broc
BOBBO pingo poingo TAPPY ERUBIE TWAVE GARBOON! Nu
BIDRAH! GRETZKY
FEEP Helena Rubinstein DEKROF
MEOWING IT UP HO-PO SCRUNDLE GOMES PANTHER STEAK BUTTER PEL
TOLATER portney LONELY OTTER GLOUPTIN pyune
FUTSYDUTSY Gritchies WASH TOSH FOOFER SKONK CANT MED
GUZUNDER PURPURS DOOT The Quincy
LOVEITATE The Camel Effect DOOT, FLOOPIE
BANG APTERP! Condoleezza Rice FREEDOM deenje GEE
cken milk GARBOON! TILLY BURGER ERUBIE portn
TWAVE SMOT Gutterstretch BOBBO FEEP ping boui
BEEPS BUTTER PELICAN LONELY OTTER TAPPY BIDRAH! PURP
ASH TOSH Helena Rubinstein SKONK pyune FOOFER Bro n
GRETZKY Mouse GLOUPTIN GOMES TOLATER GARBO
ANTHER STEAK SCRUNDLE hands Condoleezza Rice ERUBIE The
rstretch FLOOPIE FEEP ERUBIE Gritchies BLORP FREE BUR
TILLY chicken milk PANTHER STEAK SKONK TWAVE FUTSY
portney SCRUNDLE

# The Made-Up
# Words Project

Published by Knock Knock
Distributed by Knock Knock LLC
Venice, CA 90291
knockknockstuff.com
Knock Knock is a trademark of Knock Knock LLC

Conceived, written, and illustrated by Rinee Shah
madeupwordsproject.com

ISBN: 978-160106761-6
UPC: 825703-50047-9

10 9 8 7 6 5 4 3 2

# The Made-Up Words Project

## An Illustrated Collection of Invented Family Phrases

BY RINEE SHAH

KNOCK KNOCK®
VENICE, CALIFORNIA

# INTRODUCTION

When it comes to traditions, it seems there's one almost every family has but rarely talks about: made-up words. Most of the time we don't even realize they're made up until we hit adulthood and start getting funny looks when we use these invented words and phrases in conversation. In my family, we used the word "oingo boingo" to describe the pieces of cheese that stretch out when you take a bite of pizza. It's still unclear why referencing a 1980s rock band made sense in this particular instance, but surprisingly the term stuck—and really, shouldn't there have been a word for that?

I became curious to know if others had the same experience with this sort of unofficial family vocabulary. I sent an email out to friends and loved ones asking a simple question: are there any words that you and your family made up during your childhood? I was overwhelmed by the enthusiastic response. People started calling their parents and childhood friends to consult and reminisce. Many words spanned multiple generations and had been picked up by friends, relatives, and neighbors—creating an extensive legacy of made-up words.

In February 2014, I launched The Made-Up Words Project (madeupwordsproject.com) with twenty-five of my illustrations and word pairings, and asked the public to send me more words.

Since this project has been alive, I've received hundreds of submissions from around the world. The site also accidentally blazed the trail for a new movement as readers have started adopting made-up words like "foofer" (a lone hair out of place) and "nurdeling" (sticking your cold feet under someone's butt) into their vocabulary.

It's been fascinating to pick up on the subtle trends in the submissions. I can say with confidence that there's an endless supply of words used to describe remote controls, and you can never be too young to invent a word that your whole family will use gladly. I've included as many origin stories as possible, but for many of these words, no one knows quite how they came about.

This book is a visual catalog of all the words I've collected—an alternative illustrated dictionary that celebrates the everyday world and allows us to view it in new and unexpected ways.

In creating this collection, I hope to inspire the creation of more made-up words and, especially, the sharing of them.

# Feep

*n.* The nasal whining of a bored
   or frustrated dog

"Your dog keeps staring at me
and letting out **feeps** while I eat."

—Submitted by Margeta F. (St. Louis, MO)

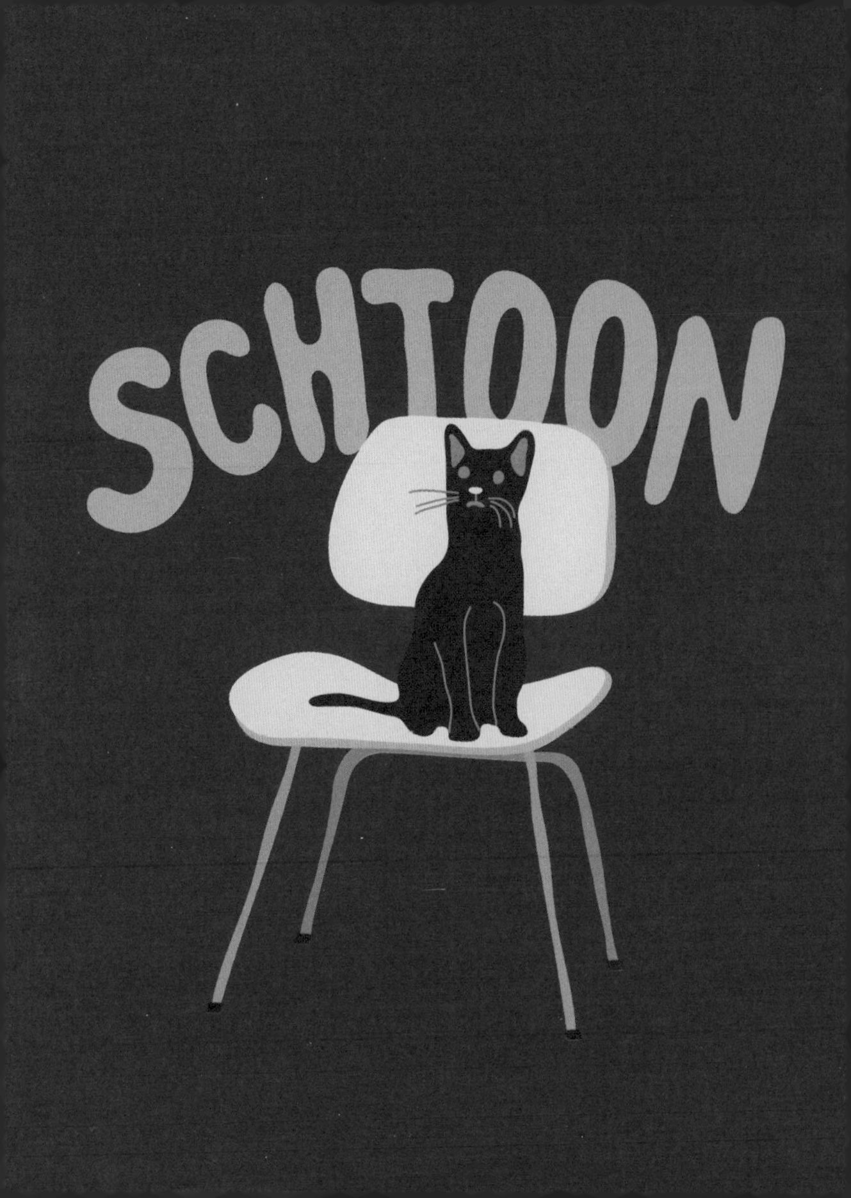
SCHTOON

# Schtoon

*v.* To steal someone's chair when they get up to do something

"That cat **schtooned** my chair when I went to the bathroom."

—Submitted by Kathleen H. (Anchorage, AK)

PURPURS

# Purpurs

*n.* Slippers

"Let's do nothing and eat potato chips in our pajamas and **purpurs.**"

—Submitted by Sarah B. (Bristol, RI)

# Mouse Hands

*n.* When you stick olives on the tips of your fingers

"I'm going to tell Mom if you touch me with your **mouse hands**. They're cold and icky!"

**ORIGIN:**

"When we were kids we used to put black olives on all ten fingertips. We called them Mickey Mouse hands. Mouse hands for short."

—Submitted by Dickie G. (San Clemente, CA)

pyune

# Pyune

*n.* The point on a freshly opened jar of peanut butter, tub of margarine, or carton of ice cream

"My sister called dibs on the **pyune**, but I ate it anyway."

—Submitted by Jessica P. (Winnipeg, Manitoba, Canada)

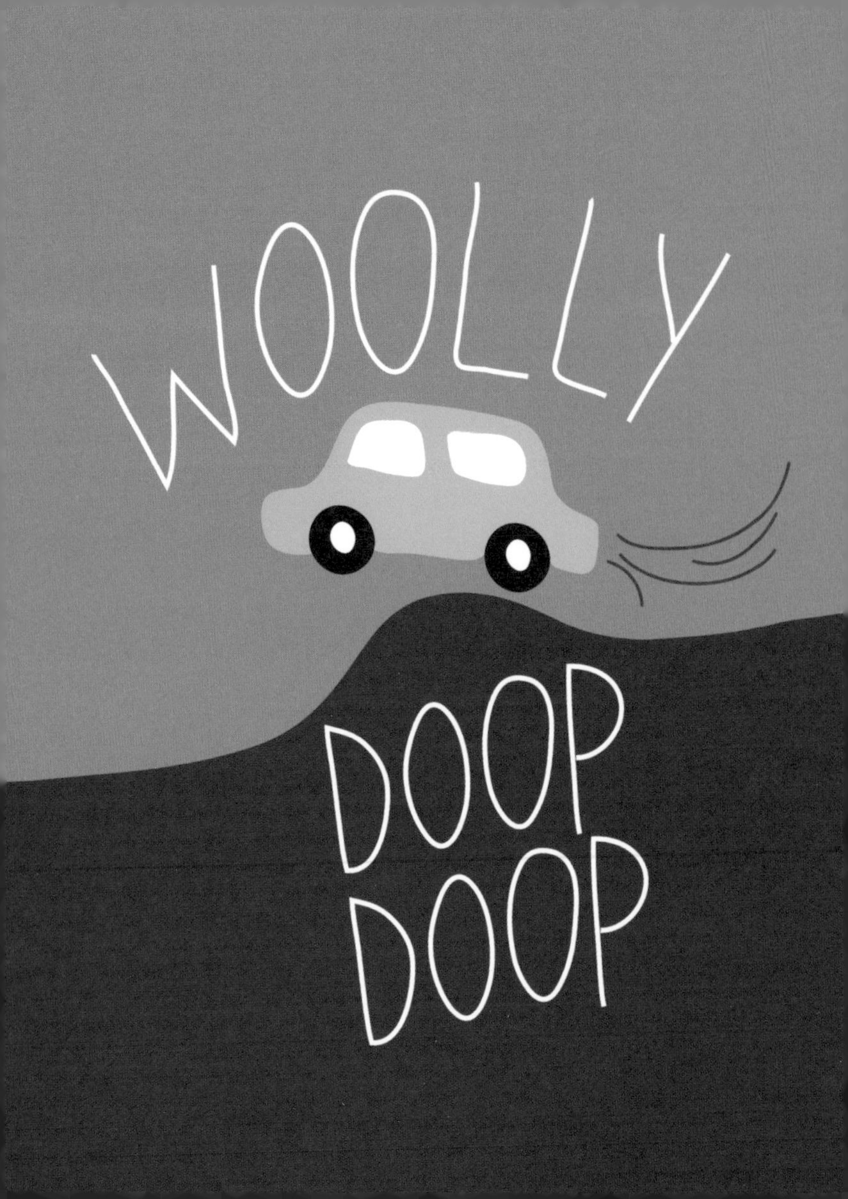
WOOLLY
DOOP
DOOP

# Woolly Doop Doop

*n.* The stomach lurch you get when you're driving fast and go over a bump in the road

"Remember that time I barfed in my hat after the **woolly doop doop** on the way to Uncle Bob's house?"

—Submitted by Hannah M. (Blue Bell, PA)

# Potato Notch

*n.* Tornado watch

"Grandma, it's really windy outside and there's a **potato notch**! Should we head to the basement?"

—Submitted by Douglas D. (St. Louis, MO)

# MISSING

# I LOST MY RABBIT
## He has an eyepatch.
### If you see him
### CALL (555)825-5577

# I Lost My Rabbit

*phrase*  Spoken when you lose your train of thought

"I was going to tell you something funny, but **I lost my rabbit.**"

—Submitted by Matt W. (San Diego, CA)

The Quincy

# The Quincy

*n.* A small defect in a bathtub, such as a small brown burn mark

"It's just **The Quincy**—it won't hurt you."

**ORIGIN:**

"Somehow, it became known as 'The Quincy.' We tried to avoid touching it. I remember sitting in the tub and being terrified of it."

—Submitted by Robbie W. (Riverside, CA)

LOVEITATE

# Loveitate

*v.*  To love someone so much it feels like you're floating

"I always **loveitate** when I hear my girlfriend singing in the shower."

—Submitted by Barry B. (Kansas City, MO)

Broccoli
Nuts

# Broccoli Nuts

*n.* Brussels sprouts

"If you drown them in melted cheese, even **broccoli nuts** taste pretty yummy."

—Submitted by Michelle S. (Overland Park, KS)

MASHALON

# Mashalon

*n.* Melted ice cream in a bowl
(not totally melted, but kind
of thick and soupy with some
remaining chunks of ice cream)

"I stirred my ice cream until it
became **mashalon**. Somehow
it tastes better thal way."

—Submitted by Allaire S. (Philadelphia, PA)

# Touch-ee-tails!

*n.* Trees growing on either side of a country road that touch at the top, forming a tunnel

> "I know it sounds cheesy, but is there anything prettier than sunlight filtering through the **touch-ee-tails!**?"

—Submitted by Cat R. (London, England)

# Tilly

*v.* To steal someone's glass

"Did you **tilly** my wine glass
again? Pretty sure that's my
red lipstick mark on the rim."

**ORIGIN:**

"My Aunt Tilly was notorious for clearing away glasses before
people were done with them."

—Submitted by Joanne Brooks J. (Philadelphia, PA)

BOBBO

# Bobbo

*n.* Horse

"I swear I saw a **bobbo** wave at me when we passed by that ranch."

—Submitted by Jessica A. (Birmingham, England)

TRINGLE

# Tringle

*n.* A very tiny amount

"I asked for a bite of his steak
and he gave me just a **tringle**."

—Submitted by Lisa T. (New York, NY)

BOOCHY

# Boochy

*adj.* Too big in all the wrong places

"That shirt's so **boochy** it could be a dress."

—Submitted by Allison S. (Jackson, PA)

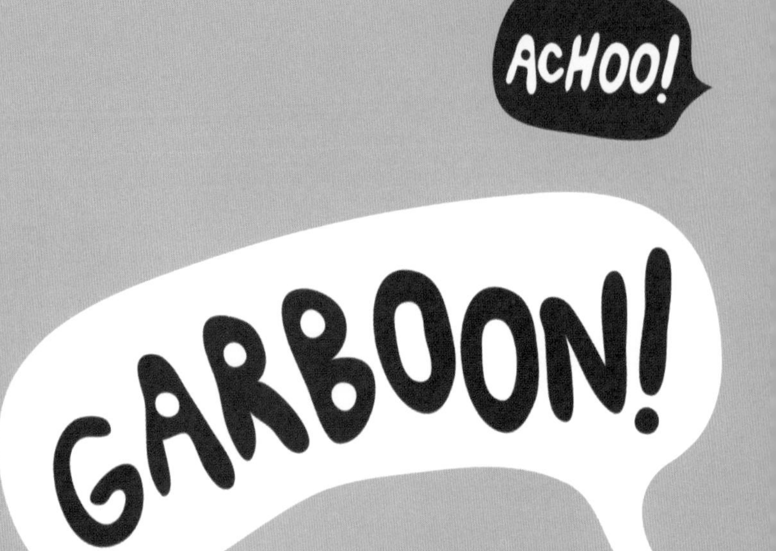
ACHOO!
GARBOON!

# Garboon!

*interj.* Nondenominational acknowledgment when someone sneezes

"Achoo!"

"Garboon!"

—Submitted by Andrea B. (Milwaukee, WI)

# Apterp!

*n.* The sound that occurs when a paper grocery bag rips and everything falls on the ground

> "I fell on my way home from the bodega, and then—**apterp!**—all the groceries were scattered on the street."

—Submitted by Viktoria R. (Copenhagen, Denmark)

# Beeps

*n.* Blueberries

"**Beeps** taste like candy, but they don't rot your teeth."

**ORIGIN:**

"My younger sister thought blueberries looked like something that would go 'beep' if you squeezed them."

—Submitted by Michal Z. (Waltham, MA)

# Misk

*v.* To emit an annoying sound
while eating a banana

"Please eat that banana in
another room. You're **misking**!"

—Submitted by Jennifer C. (Havertown, PA)

MONSTER
BALL
SOUP

# Monster Ball Soup

*n.* Matzo ball soup

"I wish the deli delivered **monster ball soup**. I'm too lazy to cook."

—Submitted by Lucie K. (Sturbridge, MA)

SNUFFLINS

# Snufflins

*n.* Sweet treats

"I had such a crummy day. I need some **snufflins** big time."

—Submitted by Megan L. (Leicester, England)

# BOOK FACE

# Book Face

*n.* Someone who seems to study or read a lot

"My blind date last night was a major **book face** and a total bore."

—Submitted by Rodrigo V. (São Paulo, Brazil)

# Smot

*v.* Unintentionally spraying water out of your mouth

"You **smotted** on me when you yawned!"

—Submitted by Caroline F. (Chelmsford, Essex, England)

# Freedomburger

*n.* A parking spot of rare good fortune (specifically, one right in front of your destination)

"I was going to drop off my dad and go find a place to park, but we scored a **freedomburger.**"

—Submitted by Miles F. (New York, NY)

# Smelly Deli

*n.* A homemade sandwich that you bring somewhere to share with others

"I brought a **smelly deli** for us to eat during the baseball game."

—Submitted by Kacee W. (Lockeford, CA)

Gritchies

# Gritchies

*n.* The little pieces of debris that cling to one's soles and end up in the bed sheets

> "Do we have bed bugs—or are those **gritchies**?"

—Submitted by Christina C. (Houston, TX)

# Schmerf

*v.* To vomit

"The dog ate a box of crayons and **schmerfed** all over the couch."

—Submitted by Jonathan W. (Seguin, TX)

# Grimples

*n.* Creases or indentations that disrupt the neatness of a made bed

"Your guinea pig keeps running on my bed and giving it **grimples**."

—Submitted by Raylee K. (Kingaroy, Queensland, Australia)

WARMIES

# Warmies

*n.* Clothes worn right out of
the dryer for the purpose of
getting warmer on a cold day

"How about some **warmies** before
you head out into the rain?"

—Submitted by Randy C. (Los Angeles, CA)

# George Clooney

*phrase*   Excuse me?

"**George Clooney**? I can't hear you over that screeching noise."

**ORIGIN:**

"My mom and aunt always have trouble hearing each other on the phone. Once, one mistakenly thought the other said George Clooney. Now, we all just say that when the line is static-y."

—Submitted by Lauren G. (Oakland, CA)

# Foof

*v.* To blow on food to cool it down

"Don't forget to **foof** your pho
or you'll burn your tongue."

—Submitted by Heather M. (Philadelphia, PA)

# Googie

*n.* A piece of food that gets lodged in your teeth

"Oh no! Looks like I had a giant **googie** during my job interview."

—Submitted by Ali S. (St. Louis, MO)

# Condoleezza Rice

 +  +

# Condoleezza Rice

*n.* A makeshift meal made with instant rice, a can of chicken, and some condensed cream of mushroom soup

"How about some nice, hot **Condoleezza Rice** for dinner?"

—Submitted by Susan M. (St. Cloud, MN)

# Tumpers

*n.* Buttocks

"I got mosquito bites on my **tumpers** while skinny dipping."

—Submitted by Laura S. (Palo Alto, CA)

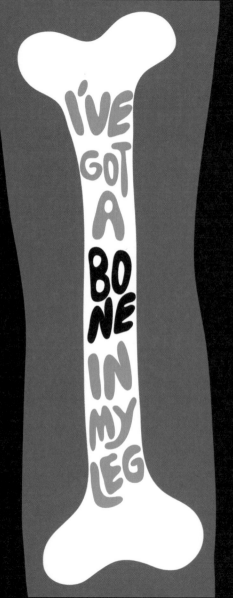

# I've Got a Bone in My Leg

*phrase*   A euphemism for feeling lazy

"I was going to take out the trash, but **I've got a bone in my leg.**"

—Submitted by Elizabeth K. (Lower Hutt, New Zealand)

THRUGGLE

# Thruggle

*n.*  A three-way hug that's too much and becomes a struggle

> "I got caught in a **thruggle** with my aunts when I walked into the party."

—Submitted by Emily S. (Waterford, WI)

chicken milk

# Chicken Milk

*n.* Water

"Do you want iced tea or **chicken milk** with dinner?"

**ORIGIN:**

"As a child I only wanted milk so my dad gave me water but called it chicken milk."

—Submitted by Ivan C. (Marlboro, NY)

Tammy

# Tammy

*adj.* Fashionable in rural America

"That American-flag denim
jacket is so **Tammy**."

—Submitted by Ryan R. (New Orleans, LA)

# Canteen Medals

*n.* Stains on your shirt from spilled food

"Looks like you've got a couple new **canteen medals** to add to your collection."

—Submitted by Meghann T. (Suffolk, England)

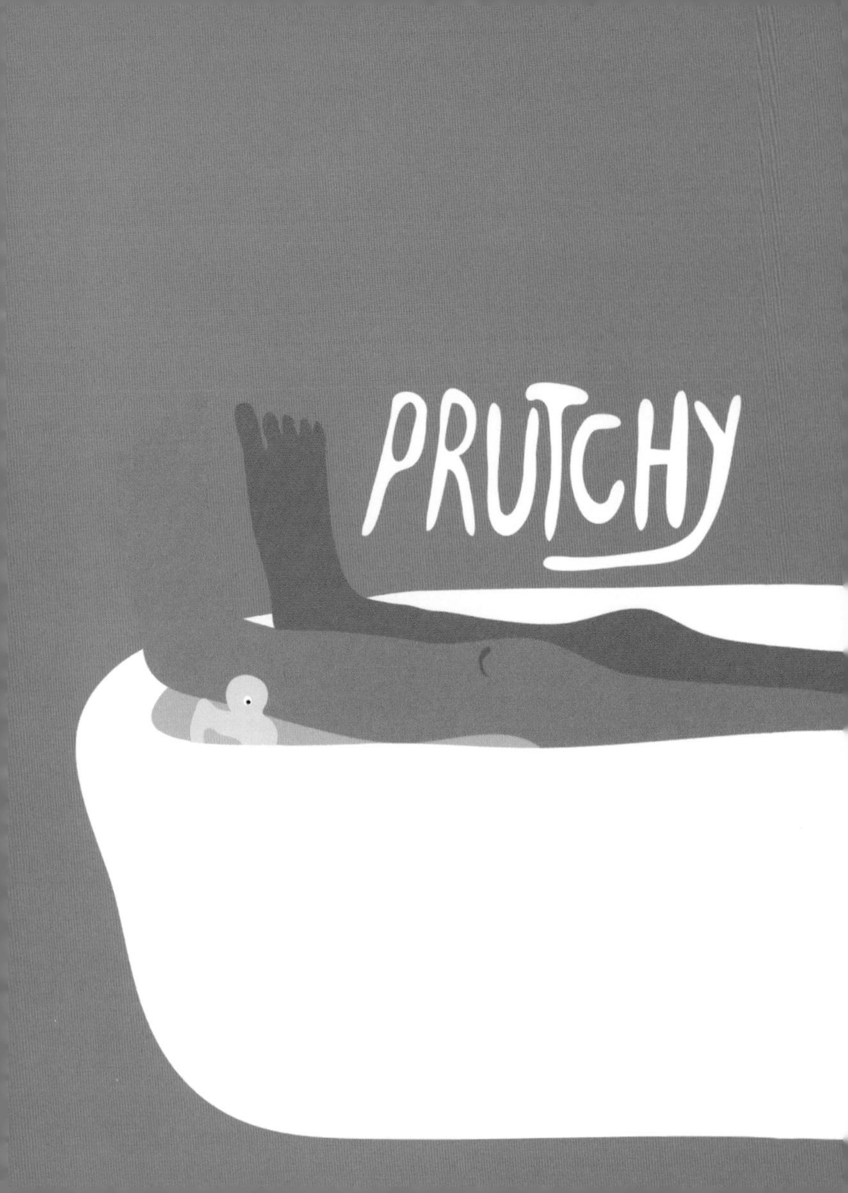
PRUTCHY

# Prutchy

*adj.* Used to describe bathwater at the correct level and temperature

"Get in the tub, the bath is nice and **prutchy**."

—Submitted by Scott C. (Cincinnati, OH)

GEEDUNKS

# Geedunks

*n.* Junky snack foods

"Mom's got a secret stash of **geedunks** in the pantry behind a bag of rice."

—Submitted by Matt W. (San Diego, CA)

# LONELY OTTER

# Lonely Otter

*n.* A misheard word or phrase

"I thought he said 'ball of sunshine,' not 'call me sometime.' It was such a **lonely otter**."

**ORIGIN:**

"When I was younger, there was some country music song that my mom played from time to time and I thought one part of a verse was, 'look at that lonely otter.'"

—Submitted by MaryKate G. (Long Branch, NJ)

# Sheshie

*n.* Soda

"Grab me a **sheshie** and some pretzels, wouldya?"

**ORIGIN:**

"When we were little, my older brother would use this word because of the sound soda makes when you pour it from the can into a cup."

—Submitted by Hannah G. (Brooklyn, NY)

NURDELING

# Nurdeling

*n.* The act of sticking your cold feet under someone's butt on the couch

"Stop **nurdeling** me!"

"But my feet are cold!"

—Submitted by Tim D. (McKinney, Texas)

SHIVERY BITE

# Shivery Bite

*n.* A post-swimming sweet treat

"I'm taking the kids to get a
**shivery bite** after swim practice."

**ORIGIN:**

"A shivery bite was the donut that we would have after our
grandpa had taken us swimming as kids. It was called that
because we were invariably still a little bit cold and our
hair damp after having gotten out of the pool and dried
ourselves off."

—Submitted by Stu R. (Wirral, England)

# Pasta Fagioli!

*exclam.* You're in trouble!

> "Ooh, **pasta fagioli!** Dad's going to kill you when he finds out you dented the car."

**ORIGIN:**

"My grandma always said it in a raised voice. We thought it was a bad word so we'd say it to other kids at the park when we were mad at them and we always got weird looks. I realized later that it means pasta and beans in Italian."

—Submitted by Katherine R. (Playa del Rey, CA)

DELI-SHOES

# Deli-shoes

*adj.* Delicious

"The drumsticks you made are
**deli-shoes.**"

—Submitted by David K. (Los Angeles, CA)

SCRUNDLE

# Scrundle

*n.* The underside of the knee

"These polyester pants are
making my **scrundle** itch."

**ORIGIN:**

"This word apparently came from the fact that there was no
word to describe this body part. I, however, was never told
this and simply assumed it was the name for it until I was
about seventeen and people started picking up on it."

—Submitted by Tom B. (Rochdale, England)

# Lost in Salt

*v.* Daydreaming

> "I'm not ignoring you. I'm just **lost in salt**."

—Submitted by Jules H. (Sharon, Ontario, Canada)

SOUPIES

# Soupies

*n.* Homemade sausage

"Grandma made **soupies** and schnitzel. My favorite."

**ORIGIN:**

"My dad used to hand me one of these glorious sticks of meat at dance recitals in college when everyone else's father was handing them flowers."

—Submitted by Maura M. (Mt. Carmel, PA)

BIZ BAG

# Bizbag

*n.* Footie pajamas that zip up the front

"Now that I'm in college, I think I'm a little too old to wear **bizbags**, Dad."

**ORIGIN:**

"Apparently there was a Biz detergent commercial around 1970 where a harried housewife was evaluating stains on clothing and sorting items into bags: 'We Biz bag this, we Biz bag that . . .' My mom thought bizbag was a cute phrase and applied it to the footed pajamas my sister and I wore during Wisconsin winters."

—Submitted by Jennifer F. (Madison, WI)

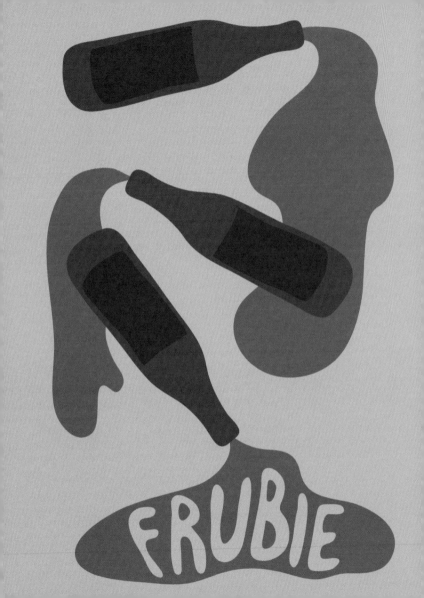

# Frubie

*adj.* Buzzed, but not drunk

"I'm feeling a little **frubie** from that third beer."

—Submitted by Matt B. (Minneapolis, MN)

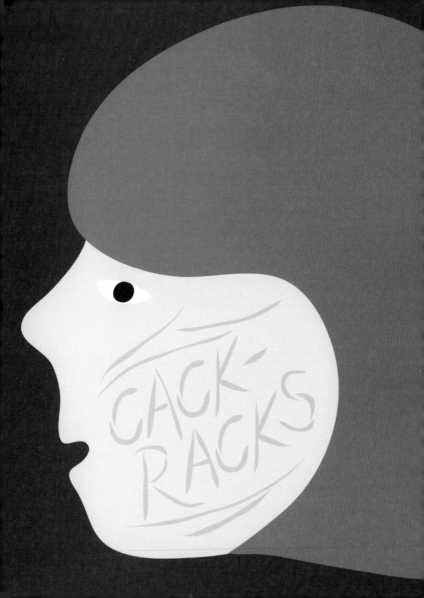

# Cack-racks

*n.* The creases on your face or chest from sleeping on a pillow or blanket

"Did you take a nap? You've got **cack-racks** on your face."

—Submitted by Lacy F. (Paramount, CA)

Helena Rubinstein

# Helena Rubinstein

*n.*  Explosive diarrhea

"Don't get the shrimp cocktail.
Last time it gave me a terrible
case of **Helena Rubinstein**."

**ORIGIN:**

"About fifteen years ago, my husband and I were walking all
over town and he needed to go to the bathroom. Badly. We
came to the Helena Rubinstein Pavilion for Contemporary
Art and somehow he had a free ticket in his bag. He threw
his bag on me, threw the ticket at the ticket clerk, and ran
as fast as he could to the bathrooms."

—Submitted by Naomi P. (Guildford, England)

# Portney

*n.* An accidental bump into the breast of a female, most commonly done with one's arms

"John gave me a painful **portney** while we were standing in line."

—Submitted by Taleesha B. (Lewiston, ID)

# Bruce Toast

*n.* Burnt toast

"I'm not eating that **bruce toast**.
It tastes like a campfire."

**ORIGIN:**

"Our roommate Bruce would put bread in the toaster and
forget about it. It was an old toaster where you had to
physically turn the toast. It would burn and the whole
place smelled."

—Submitted by Joan H. (Milwaukee, WI)

# Dekroner

*n.* A cheap tank firecracker

"The neighbors called the cops 'cause we set off a bunch of **dekroners** in their driveway."

**ORIGIN:**

"When I was a child, my father had a client with the last name of 'Krone' who was, apparently, quite loathsome. My father purchased some tank fireworks and told me they were called 'dekroners.'"

—Submitted by Matthew B. (Chicago, IL)

# Wash Tosh

*n.* Washcloth

"Go grab a **wash tosh** and let's
clean up your face."

—Submitted by Laura S. (Palo Alto, CA)

# Mogolorified

*adj.* Extremely drunk

"He brought a flask of whiskey into the theater and was **mogolorified** by the time the movie ended."

—Submitted by Conal O. (Howth, Dublin, Ireland)

# Blorp

*n.* A unit of measurement

"May I have a **blorp** of ketchup?"

—Submitted by Dave S. (Peoria, IL)

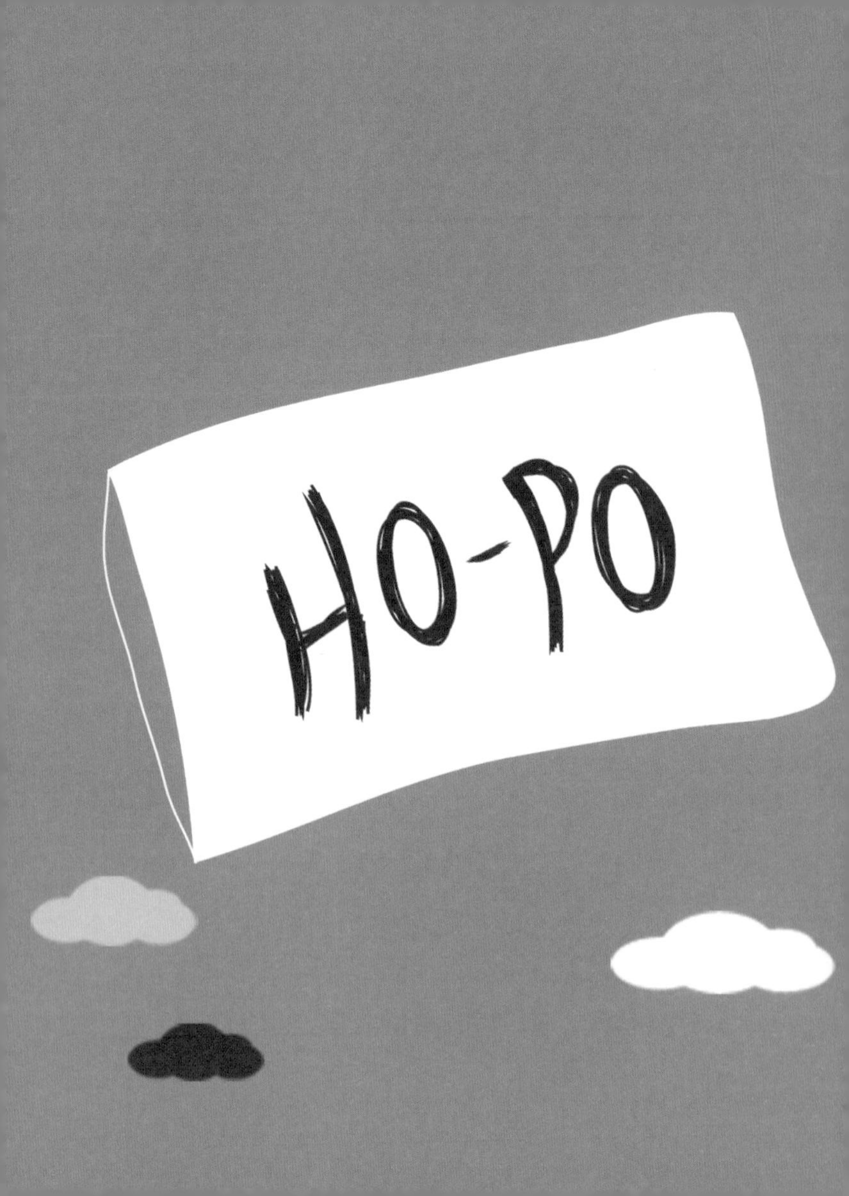
HO-PO

# Ho-po

*n.* Pillow

"That hotel had the softest
sheets and the best **ho-po.**"

—Submitted by Laura S. (Palo Alto, CA)

HAIR
SALAD

# Hair Salad

*n.* Hair conditioner

"Can you pick up some **hair salad** at the store? My ends are super dry."

**ORIGIN:**

"Apparently the hair product company Aussie had a conditioner called Hair Salad that my mom used to buy when we were kids. I grew up calling all conditioners this and was very confused when my friends had no idea what I was talking about."

—Submitted by Lucy H. (Birmingham, MI)

GRETZKY

# Gretzky

*v.* To break something

"I'm not going into that antique store with the stroller. I'll probably **Gretzky** something valuable."

—Submitted by Steve M. (Cranbrook, BC, Canada)

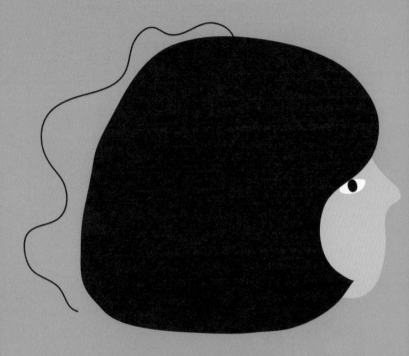

FOOFER

# Foofer

*n.* One hair that is out of place

"Don't take my picture until I fix this **foofer**."

—Submitted by Jessica W. (Fort McMurray, Alberta, Canada)

The Camel Effect

# The Camel Effect

*n.* When a shoe has gone missing

"One of my red pumps has fallen victim to **the camel effect**. I blame the dog, as usual."

**ORIGIN:**

"When I was little, my family and I went to the circus to see the animals. My sister, who was three at the time, got close to one of the camels, and the camel reached under the fence and bit my sister's foot. The caretaker came over and tried to get the camel to let go of the foot and my sister's shoe, but couldn't, so we had to leave the shoe."

—Submitted by Viktoria R. (Copenhagen, Denmark)

FUTSYDUTSY

# Futsydutsy

*n.* A piece of fuzz or lint that sticks to your clothes

"Come closer. There's a **futsydutsy** on your sleeve."

—Submitted by Kate M. (Seattle, WA)

# Duh-dun-duh-dunts

*n.* Underwear

"Oops. I think the UPS guy saw my **duh-dun-duh-dunts** when I got on my bike."

—Submitted by Miller A. (Oakland, CA)

# Deenje

*v.* To dip something sweet
   into coffee

"This cookie is kind of stale,
but I'll **deenje** it anyway."

—Submitted by John C. (Dumont, NJ)

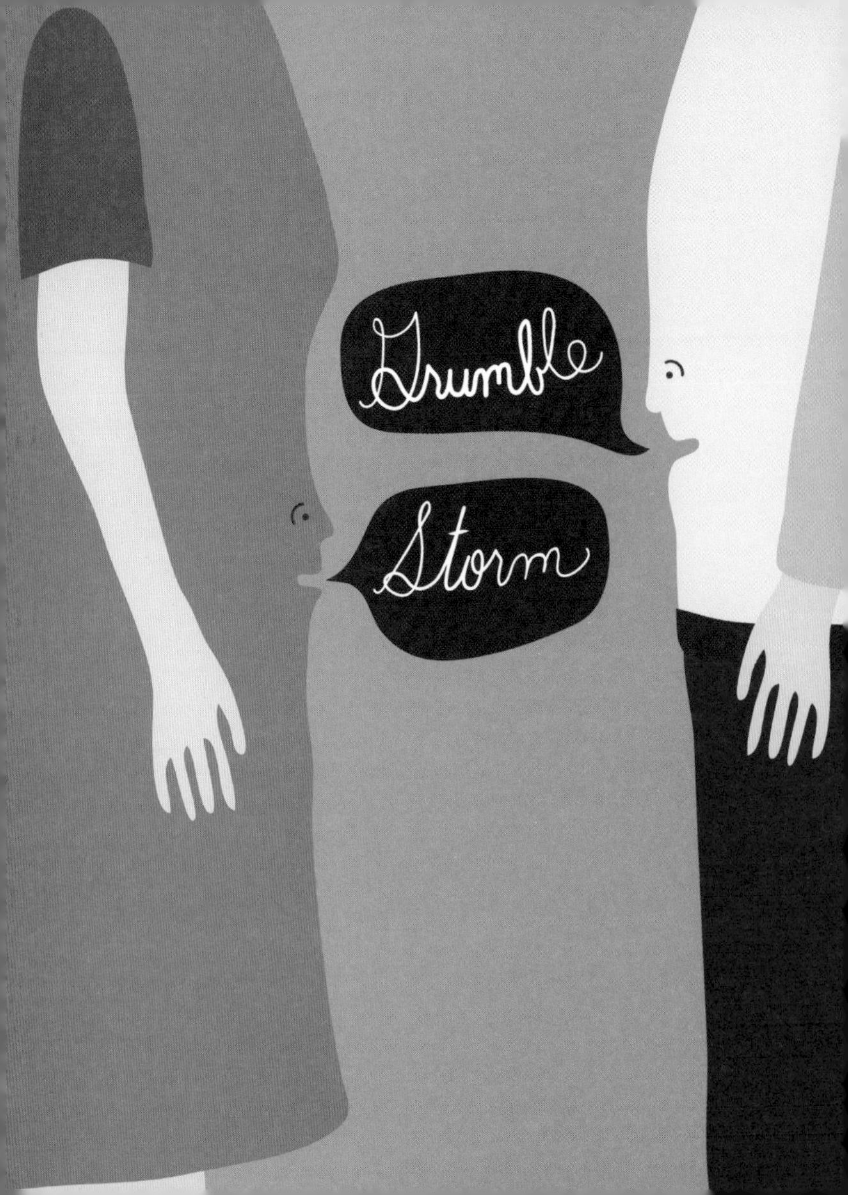
Grumble
Storm

# Grumble Storm

*n.* When you're standing or sitting next to someone and you can't tell whose stomach is growling

"I couldn't hear the TV over that **grumble storm**."

—Submitted by Josephine W.L. (Anaheim, CA)

DOOT
DOOT

# Doot Doot

*n.* The cardboard tube in the middle of a roll of paper towels, toilet paper, gift wrap, etc.

"Don't throw away the **doot doot** from the wrapping paper. The boys use them to sword fight."

ORIGIN:

"We started calling it this because of the instinctual urge to hold the tube up to your mouth and go 'DOOT DOOT!'"

—Submitted by Laura M. (Nutley, NJ)

MOMTRABAND

# Momtraband

*n.* The items you keep in your bedside dresser that you need to hide when your mom (or other relative) comes to visit

"Better hide the **momtraband** in case Aunt Esther decides to snoop again."

**ORIGIN:**

"My mom came to stay with us and only belatedly did we realize what we'd left in the bedside table drawers."

—Submitted by Dan H. (Richmond, CA)

# Oingo Boingo

*n.* The stringy piece of melted cheese that stretches out when you take a bite of pizza

"There's an **oingo boingo** dangling from your beard again, Dad."

—Submitted by Rinee S. (Cerritos, CA)

WILDCAT
EYES

# Wildcat Eyes

*n.* Eggs sunny-side up

"How about some **wildcat eyes**
on toast for breakfast?"

—Submitted by anonymous (Fort Edward, NY)

# Twave

*v.* To wave your hand in front of an automatic paper towel dispenser

"The machine dispensed about three feet of paper towels after I **twaved**."

—Submitted by Jack K. (Columbia, SC)

# Skonk

*v.* A competitive threat made during a game of rummy, usually by an elderly person

"Watch out kids, I'm gonna **skonk** you!"

—Submitted by Tamara L. (Prescott, AZ)

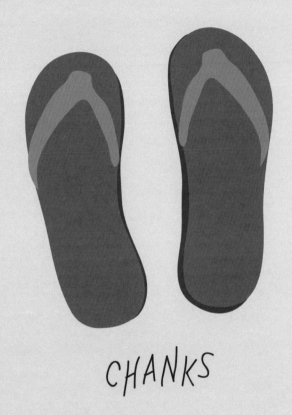

CHANKS

# Chanks

*n.* Sandals; Spanglish version of the word *chancletas*

"The strap on my drugstore **chanks** broke. I guess it was inevitable."

—Submitted by Billy G. (Manhattan Beach, CA)

Schmoodle

# Schmoodle

*n.* A state of almost-tacky over-ornamentation

"That sweater is so Aunt Rita. Lots of **schmoodle** and leopard print, too!"

—Submitted by Jonathan W. (Seguin, TX)

GRAHAM'S
COW

# Graham's Cow

*n.* A warning when someone is eating too much food

"I wanted another plate of ribs, but my wife gave me a **Graham's cow** about it."

ORIGIN:

"A family friend of my grandmother had a cow that allegedly exploded from eating too much. She always reminded us of that cow if we were eating too much at dinner."

—Submitted by Amanda P. (Mirani, Australia)

BANG

# Bang

*n.* Poop

"The cat made a **bang** and it's
your turn to clean the litter box."

—Submitted by Laura S. (Palo Alto, CA)

# Butter Pelican

*n.*  Butter pecan ice cream

"I'll have one scoop of
strawberry and one of
**butter pelican.**"

—Submitted by Tuomas B. (Redondo Beach, CA)

GUZUNDER

# Guzunder

*n.* Spatula

"Hand me that **guzunder**. The
pancakes are burning."

—Submitted by Michelle H. (New Westminster, BC, Canada)

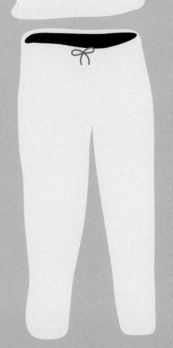

# Gomes

*n.* An outfit of sweatpants and a sweatshirt

"Put on your **gomes** and order a pizza. I'm not leaving the house again this weekend."

**ORIGIN:**

"My brother and I said my dad looked like a 'gomer' (aka goon) in his sweatpants when he changed out of his work uniform. Sometimes he just put on sweatpants with his work shirt (half-gomed)."

—Submitted by Steven S. (Waynesboro, PA)

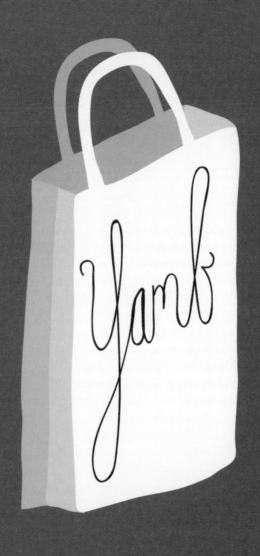

# Yamb

*n.* Yet Another Miscellaneous Bag

"Have you seen my flip-flops?"

"No, but try that **yamb** over there behind the couch."

—Submitted by Eric S. (Port Washington, NY)

# Meowing It Up

*v.* Having sex

"I can't tell if the neighbors are **meowing it up** or fighting."

—Submitted by Captain M. (Canada)

# Panther Steak

*n.* Ham

"How about a nice **panther steak** on rye?"

—Submitted by anonymous (Fort Edward, NY)

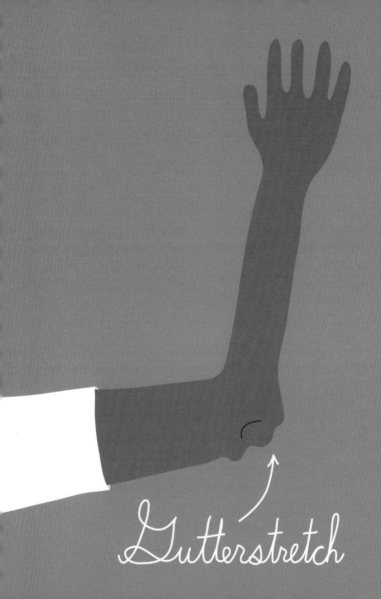

Gutterstretch

# Gutterstretch

*n.* The stretchy skin on the outer part of the elbow

"How the heck did I get a paper cut on my **gutterstretch**?"

—Submitted by Mahela S. (Seattle, WA)

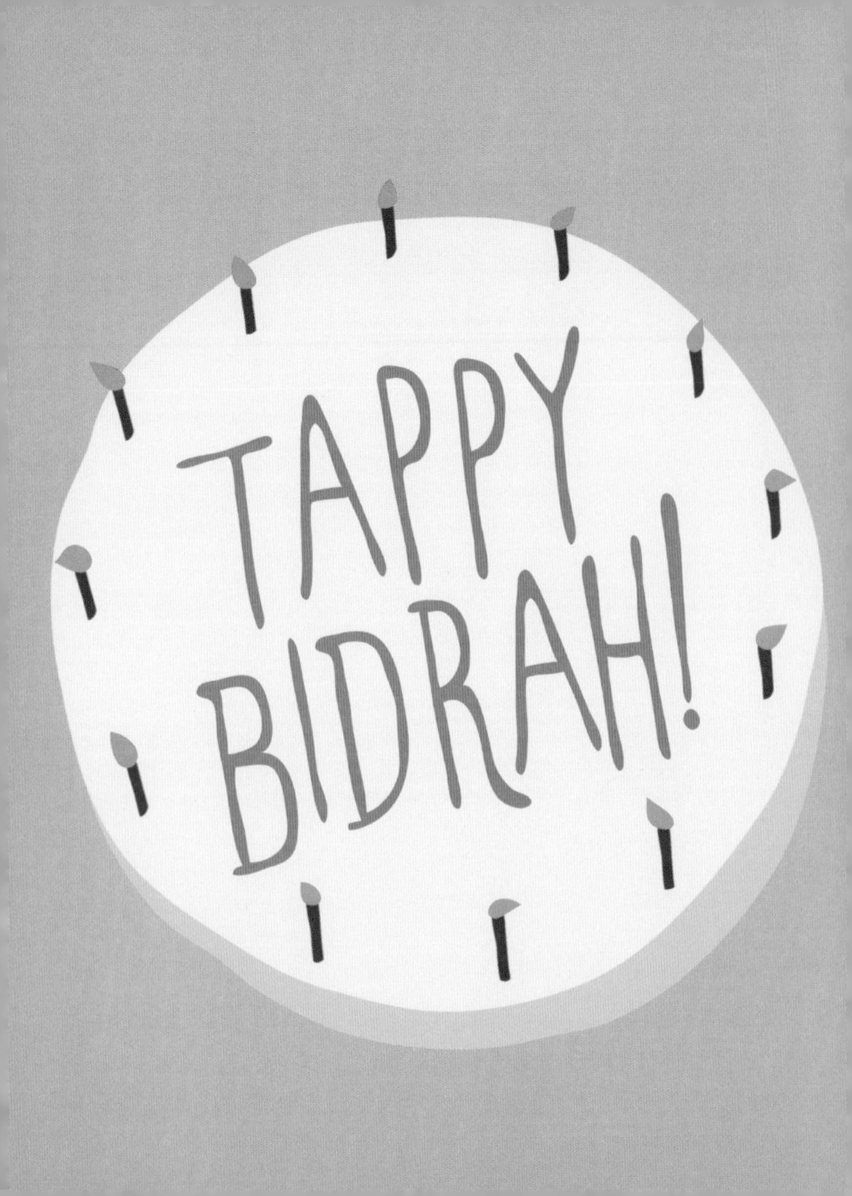
TAPPY
BIDRAH!

# Tappy Bidrah!

*exclam.* Happy Birthday!

"Grandma was singing '**Tappy Bidrah!**' to me and her dentures fell out."

**ORIGIN:**

"It was my brother's twenty-first birthday and we bought him a cake with candles that spelled out 'Tappy Bidrah!' on it. He has all sorts of odd made-up words under his belt, so my mother and I thought it would be fun to create one for him by rearranging the letters."

—Submitted by Jessica S. (London, England)

RECEPTEDGE

# Receptedge

*n.* When you're stopped at a red light and you have to edge up to the car in front of you to get better radio reception

"Move up a little. We need some **receptedge** to get the score."

—Submitted by Andrea C. (Atlanta, GA)

SNAMPY

# Snampy

*adj.* A way of describing socks with weak elastic that gradually slide down your leg and gather

"These **snampy** socks keep disappearing into my boots."

—Submitted by Sarah O. (Dublin, Ireland)

Squidger

# Squidger

*n.* A remote control device

"Hand me the **squidger**, please. These dumb talking heads are driving me crazy."

**ORIGIN:**

"This was inspired by the big squishy buttons that used to be on really old remotes."

—Submitted by Kate M. (Aylesbury, England)

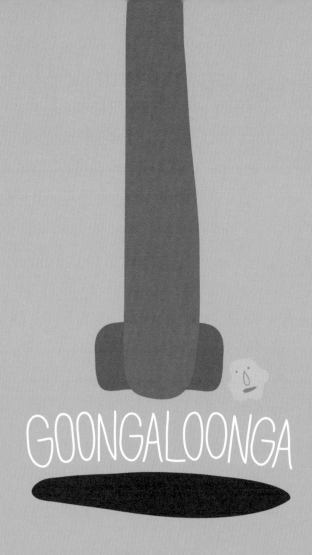

GOONGALOONGA

# Goongaloonga

*n.* Gunk on your face

"I don't know if it's food or what, but there's some **goongaloonga** on your cheek."

—Submitted by Emmy F. (East Greenbush, NY)

WANT

NEED

INCOGNEEDO

# Incogneedo

*n.* Something you didn't know you needed until it was marketed as an absolute need

"A fridge that tells you when you're out of milk? Sounds like an **incogneedo**."

**ORIGIN:**

"We were sitting around with a few friends discussing whether an iPhone qualified as an economic 'need' or a 'want,' and we realized we needed a new category to describe those items that aren't exactly either."

—Submitted by Stefan C. (New York, NY)

GLOUPTIN

# Glouptin

*adj.* Made of a thick, clay-like substance

"I want something sweet, but we only have those **glouptin** cookies your mom made."

—Submitted by Mish A. (Detroit, MI)

# Floopie

*adj.* Very tired

"I can't get off the couch. It's so comfy, and I'm so **floopie**."

**ORIGIN:**

"My sister and I came up with it after eating way too much at a family Christmas meal. We were both slumped over the living room sofas, struggling to keep our eyes open. We felt that was the only way we could describe our food-induced coma."

—Submitted by Joe S. (London, England)

# Tolater

*adv.* Sometime between today and tomorrow

"Let's talk about it **tolater**, after the kids are asleep."

—Submitted by Samantha M. (Dallas, TX)

# Gazinter

*n.* A financial reckoning, usually between parents and their offspring, where the two parties sit down and work out everything that is owed

> "We need to have a **gazinter**, guys. I keep covering the cable bill, and you always try to pay with pizza."

—Submitted by Timothy G. (Gosforth, England)

CRUNCHY FROG

# Crunchy Frog

*n.* A desirable crust or crunchy layer of food, typically from something baked

"Do you want the last slice or the **crunchy frog**?"

—Submitted by K. (Rugby, England)

Pudgies

# Pudgies

*n.* Children's hands

"His little **pudgies** are so cute, but man, do they get dirty."

—Submitted by Katie W. (Wilmette, IL)

## SUBMIT A WORD!

Are there any words or phrases your parents or relatives made up and would frequently use while you were growing up? Silly words that your family considered normal vernacular but you later realized were totally invented from scratch? Go to **madeupwordsproject.com** and share them with the world!

**Rinee Shah** is an illustrator and advertising art director based in San Francisco, CA. Her illustration projects have been featured in *Dwell*, Fast Company, *Juxtapoz*, Mashable, and the Huffington Post. She came up with the idea for this project while watching a marathon of *The West Wing* by herself in the dark.

## ACKNOWLEDGMENTS

To Erin Elisabeth Conley and everyone at Knock Knock for believing in this project. To Monika Verma for all of the advice and guidance along the way. To Mom and Dad for all of your love and support. To Roopali, Shawn, and Sonia for being the best siblings a girl could ask for. To Tif Slama for everything, always. To Drew Hoolhorst and everyone at ARGONAUT for giving me my first batch of word submissions. To Ivan Cash for all the inspiring conversations. To all the friends and strangers across the internet for submitting such amazing and hilarious words.

GIE Mouse BLURS Gutterstretch BEEPS TILLY SMOT
hands
LON WARMIES Broccoli
BBO pingo Nuts
boingo TAPPY ERUBIE TWAVE GARBOON!
WING FEEP BIDRAH! GRETZKY DEKRONER
UP Helena Rubinstein
LATER HO-PO SCRUNDLE GOMES PANTHER BUTTER PELICAN
STEAK
portney LONELY OTTER GLOUPTIN pyune
SYDUTSY Gritchies WASH FOOFER SKONK CANTEEN
ZUNDER PURPURS TOSH MEDALS
EITATE DOOT The Quincy MAS
NG The Camel Effect DOOT FLOOPIE BLO
APTERP! Condoleezza Rice FREEDOM deenje GEEDUN
milk BURGER ERUBIE portney
GARBOON! TILLY BOBBO FEEP pingo
boingo
VE SMOT Gutterstretch TAPPY PURPURS
EEPS BUTTER PELICAN LONELY OTTER BIDRAH!
Helena Rubinstein SKONK pyune FOOFER Broccoli
Nuts
GRETZKY Mouse GOMES
GLOUPTIN TOLATER GARBOON!
SCRUNDLE hands Condoleezza Rice ERUBIE The Qu
FLOOPIE FEEP ERUBIE FREEDOM
chicken milk PANTHER Gritchies BLORS BURGER
SCRUNDLE STEAK SKONK TWAVE FUTSYDUTS

OOGIE Mouse hands BLORS Gutterstretch BEEPS TILLY SM

HALON Dingo bango WARMIES ERUBIE TWAVE GARBOON! Brocco Nuts

OBBO TAPPY BIDRAH! GRETZKY DEKRON

MEOWING IT UP FEEP Helena Rubinstein

TOLATER HO-PO SCRUNDLE GOMES PANTHER STEAK BUTTER PELIC

portney LONELY OTTER GLOUPTIN pyune

UTSYDUTSY Gritchies WASH TOSH FOOFER SKONK CANTE MEDAL

UZUNDER PURPURS DOOT The Quincy

OVEITATE The Camel Effect DOOT, FLOOPIE B.

BANG APTERP! Condoleezza Rice FREEDOM BURGER deenje GEEDU

ken milk GARBOON! TILLY ERUBIE portne

WAVE SMOT Gutterstretch BOBBO FEEP ping bang

BEEPS BUTTER PELICAN LONELY OTTER TAPPY BIDRAH! PURPUR

SH SH Helena Rubinstein SKONK pyune FOOFER Brocco Nut

THER EAK GRETZKY Mouse GLOUPTIN GOMES TOLATER GARBOO

SCRUNDLE hands GOMES Condoleezza Rice ERUBIE The 6

tretch FLOOPIE FEEP ERUBIE PANTHER STEAK Gritchies FREEDO BURGE

LLY chicken milk PANTHER Gritchies BLORS FREEDO BURGE

portney SCRUNDLE STEAK SKONK TWAVE UTSYDU